"Once we push through the curtain of fear,
we find our dreams on the other side."

# 20/20 Vision
# Dreams

## List of 100 Dreams

### GARNET THOMPSON

20/20 Vision Dreams by Garnet Thompson
Published 2019 by Your Book Angel
Copyright © Garnet Thompson

All rights reserved. No part of this book may be reproduced, stored, or transmitted by any means—whether auditory, graphic, mechanical, or electronic—without written permission of both publisher and author, except in the case of brief excerpts used in critical articles and reviews. Unauthorized reproduction of any part of this work is illegal and is punishable by law.

The characters are all mine, any similarities with other fictional or real persons/places are coincidental.

Printed in the United States
Edited by Keidi Keating
Layout by Rochelle Mensidor

ISBN: 978-1-7330436-6-3

An interactive book and journal
focused on helping YOU the reader
to make and track progress
in living YOUR dreams.

Garnet Thompson

I would like to dedicate this book to all of the people in my life who have contributed in a positive way and spurred me on to live my dreams. Special thanks to my wife, Nadine, children, Jasmine and Anthony, and my grandmother, Mavis Leslie for being unending sources of encouragement over the years. Hope all your dreams become a reality. Make it happen (MIH) by daring to dream!

# Table of Contents

**Introduction**
*Why Dreaming Is Important* ................ 9

**Chapter One**
*The Great Journey of Life* .................. 15

**Chapter Two**
*Holding On To the Vision* ................. 29

**Chapter Three**
*The Foundation and Pillars of Life.* .......... 39

**Chapter Four**
*The Currency of Time* .................... 48

**Chapter Five**
*The Will to Persist* ....................... 60

**Chapter Six**
*The Desire to Explore Uncharted Waters* ..... 70

**Chapter Seven**
*Winds of Adversity* ...................... 80

CHAPTER EIGHT
   *Great Sailing Weather*................ 91

CHAPTER NINE
   *Excess Baggage Overboard*............ 101

CHAPTER TEN
   *Crossing Paths with Special Voyagers* ...... 115

CHAPTER ELEVEN
   *All Hands On Deck*................... 124

CHAPTER TWELVE
   *Treasure Chest of Lessons Learned* ........ 134

CHAPTER THIRTEEN
   *The Science of Dreaming*.............. 149

CHAPTER FOURTEEN
   *The End of the Voyage*................ 158

YOUR LIST OF 100 DREAMS........ 165

ABOUT THE AUTHOR ............. 199

# Introduction

# Why Dreaming Is Important

Let's start with a dictionary definition of dreams: "a series of thoughts, images, and sensations occurring in a person's mind."

Dreaming is the conscious or subconscious act of imagining the possibility of something occurring. As children, we tend to dream quite often, both during our sleep and sometimes while awake. Children are typically the greatest dreamers of new ideas and concepts which appear to be impossible or unthinkable by most adults.

As we grow up, most adults tend to lose their willingness and ability to let their minds wander and just dream. The human mind is always active whether we are asleep or awake. The thoughts which flow through our minds can be likened to a great river from an unknown source, which washes through our minds, leaving debris and residue for us to examine closer during our waking hours. The deposits of debris (images or visions) of places, people, things, and experiences which we find appealing and drawn to exploring provide a sense of hope, which is vital to maintaining the life force within our beings.

Every person has dreams, which to them seem quite large and are considered incredible if and when they are achieved. Those same dreams to another individual may appear commonplace, expected, and potentially mundane. However, each individual starts out in life from different social, economic, cultural, geographical, and political backgrounds. Whatever dreams an individual finds compelling to them can be unique or sometimes common to a large portion of the population.

A challenge faced by some young people is finding interesting and effective ways to become or stay inspired and motivated to live up to their full potential and to contribute to society in a positive way. As a parent of two children, this was a struggle I recognized was being experienced by our offspring as they approached their teenage years. It was July in the summer of 2013 and I had taken a one-week vacation from work to spend some quality time with our son and daughter. The idea floated across my mind that I should purchase two hardcover black notebooks and sit down with both our offspring to have them list out the dreams they held in their young minds.

The three of us sat down on the floor, at which time I communicated to them the instructions for a fun new game we were about to play. I asked them to think of all the things, places, experiences, and dreams they wanted to make real during the time we had off that week or many years in the future. Before we knew it, an hour had passed and both of them were eagerly thinking of and writing down all the dreams that were rushing into their minds. During that week of vacation, we selected some of the captured dreams and actively set out to make them a reality. The exercise brought big smiles and a sense of satisfaction to both our youngsters. They now had a real sense that whatever thoughts came to their minds, it would be possible to work hard enough and take deliberate stepwise actions in order to make them a reality.

These dream recording and tracking sessions became an annual summer event and every year since that time their lists of 100 dreams have been growing while dreams which have been accomplished have been checked off the list with an overwhelming sense of satisfaction. After witnessing how much this dream recording and tracking activity inspired and continues to inspire our offspring, I felt that making this activity available in a book format to other youth—who may be in unfortunate circumstances without loving parents or guardians in their corners—would be beneficial, and that such a book or journal would be of value to a specific segment of the youth population.

I also wrote this book to share some of the lessons learned during my journey through life so far with a desire to help future generations. The personal stories to be shared will range from my days of youth to more recent times as an adult with family responsibilities. The intention is to allow the reader an opportunity to have a fast-forward view into one human's life experiences and some situations faced, which may offer valuable lessons to be interpreted and applied to their own lives now or at some distant point in the future. The vision held in my heart and mind is for every young person (in physical age or at heart) to be equipped with mental tools, such as attitude, desire, persistence, and team support, and to be able to use their talents to successfully navigate the ocean of life.

By sharing some of my personal stories and adventures from the paths I have traveled, I sincerely hope to provide further insight to better equip youthful dream-seekers with a backpack of practical tools and knowledge. It is a duty, an honour, and a privilege to encourage the reader to further cultivate an attitude and mindset necessary to live their dreams. Let's dare to dream together and strive to make them all real!

# Chapter One

# The Great Journey of Life

Reality is the starting point for everyone who has a dream or multiple dreams that they want to achieve. However, the reality that some of us experience is oftentimes vastly different from the life we wish to live. Imagine that you are standing alone on the shore of a frozen (*or seemingly frozen*) lake barefoot; your mind starts to wander and you begin to see images in your mind of yourself on the other side of the lake experiencing all the things, people, situations, and happiness that you have ever dreamt of living.

After some time, your mind is dragged back to reality by a harsh sensation of pain, induced by the numbing cold coming from the ground on which your bare feet are standing. At this point you realize you now have a choice to make:

(1) Focus on solving the immediate need of warming your bare feet and forgetting about your recent vision.
(2) Immediately start to dash across the seemingly frozen water towards the other side.
(3) Focus on solving the immediate need of warming your bare feet while firmly holding onto the vision with a desire to one day get to the other side.

Every person brought into this world as a newborn baby has been set at the starting point of a great journey. The sights, sounds, smells, tastes, and things they touch or come in contact with help to shape their known reality. Whether the journey will be awful, mediocre, good, great or spectacular will be determined by the way that individual perceives the world about them. The attitude adopted by the individual either consciously or unconsciously will determine the level of success and the results along the way.

The various stages of human development from a baby, to a toddler, to a teenager then on to adulthood bring with them an array of experiences, some positive and others negative, which influence their attitudes and willingness to take risks. We learn who we think we are based on these earlier experiences and then commence to interact with the world based on these learned behaviours and assumptions.

We set out into the world after completing what we think is the educational process that will equip us for success. Some individuals realize early on that they must keep learning and developing in order to become successful and live their dreams. While many others feel they have all the knowledge necessary and avoid learning anything new, which could make the journey a lot easier, or at the very minimum, more comfortable over the decades to follow.

It is incredible to realize that each and every one of the millions of choices we make starting in our childhood will combine to determine how successful we will be for a significant portion of our lives. Human beings have the ability to examine their lives and to determine if those lives match up with the vision held in their minds. Any discrepancies revealed during these periods of self-reflection have the ability to drive the person to make changes or to accept the current fortunate or unfortunate circumstances in which they are living.

Our journey through life can take us thousands of kilometers away from the location of our birth or for some individuals, allow themselves to remain within a one-hundred-kilometer radius of their place of birth.

The need to explore new, never before seen lands drives some individuals to set out on a path of exploration never to return home again.

The people and personalities we come in contact with during our lives vary as much as the different types of fishes in the ocean. Some people come into our lives for a short time, some simply pass by without any fanfare or without being noticed, while others stay in our lives for a substantial period of time. We often fail to realize that even though it may seem that we have all the time in the world, time is actually speeding by and the people in our lives are coming and leaving at a pace that is sometimes shocking once we really open our eyes for the first time and truly notice.

There comes a time in everyone's life when the realization dawns that life is fleeting and everything and everyone about us is in a constant state of change. This realization could either drive us to greater accomplishments or paralyze us with an overwhelming sense of dread and fear. Often, at this very moment, it becomes clear that there is nothing to lose by making an all-out effort to live out the dreams and images playing on the movie screen in our minds. Every minute, hour, day, year, and decade that goes by provides us with an increased level of knowledge and experience to better equip us for the journey ahead.

Where we live and how we spend our time are in our complete control whether we believe it or not. We have a choice at any moment to make a decision to acquire new knowledge and make very slight changes or dramatic changes in our lives, which can bring a new sense of adventure and zest for life never before experienced. There is but one outcome at the end of everyone's journey through life, so it stands to reason that making the best of the precious time we have on Earth would be the wisest decision anyone could consciously choose to make.

It is fitting to compare human beings to ships navigating the vast oceans, with adventure and unknown possibilities on every side, since human beings are sailing through time unaware of all that is going on beyond their field of view at any given moment. If only we could periodically see the future and then come back to reality to live it, this would allow us to pay closer attention to the people and situations which truly matter most in our lives. The end result would be us embracing our humanity as messy as it sometimes gets, then seeking ways to provide value and to support the other humans in our lives.

In the opening paragraph of this book the image which was hopefully conjured up in your mind of yourself standing alone on the shore of a frozen (*or seemingly frozen*) lake barefoot, was used to represent an individual perhaps such as yourself, who may be on the cusp of a significant change in life. A change such as on the verge of graduating from high school, college or an institute of higher learning. The picture of being barefoot represents you being equipped with a base level of theoretical knowledge, which will be required in your life. The frozen lake represents your local community or marketplace in which you are wanting to contribute your talents and skills. However, the right connections, opportunity, time, persistence, and continued practical experience will be required to provide the necessary footwear (i.e. knowledge, understanding, and wisdom) to successfully crack the ice and make an opening or breakthrough in joining the already firmly established marketplace. Once you have further developed after graduating and made your way into the now thawed waters, in the vessel of your choice, you will then be on your way to navigate through the rivers, tributaries or waterways, which will lead you to the vast ocean of life which awaits your contributions.

The gap between our current reality and our vision is the great journey of life. We each have many choices to make in order to safely navigate to the other side and to one day experience our dreams.

## *Personal Story*

*The year 2020 will commemorate a milestone birthday. I will have been on Planet Earth for half a century or fifty years or five decades; whichever way you look at it, a significant amount of valuable time has elapsed. As Socrates said, "An unexamined life is not worth living," so it makes sense to stop and analyze the past decades with an eager eye towards the future. Some of the questions which race through my almost-fifty-year-old mind are:*

1) *Have I accomplished the dreams or things which I set out to achieve during my days of youth?*
2) *Have I made a difference or positively impacted anyone's life?*
3) *Are the things which I have accomplished meaningful to the world?*
4) *Am I the best me that I can be?*
5) *What will be my legacy?*
6) *What's next and what does the future hold?*

*My journey started out at birth on the small tropical island of Jamaica in the Caribbean Sea. At the time of writing this book my family, which consists of my wife Nadine, my son Anthony (age sixteen), my daughter*

*Jasmine (age eighteen), and myself, are living in a small town in Southern Ontario, Canada. The past decades so far have resulted in trips to a number of islands and countries to meet and interact with a variety of inhabitants of our planet.*

*At this point in life, my answer to question #1 above is a resounding YES! I have accomplished most, if not all of the personal and career dreams which were in my mind as a youth growing up in a presumed Caribbean paradise. During my youth, I dreamt of flying to distant far-off lands and experiencing other cultures and meeting new people. The idea and thought of getting on an airplane and flying as free as the birds raced through my young mind for most of my childhood days. I reasoned that if I became a pilot, I would then have unlimited opportunities to fly each and every day.*

*Over the past years, I have had the opportunity to board many flights (as a passenger) and to travel to lands around the globe, which are located north, south, east, and west of Jamaica. I think my younger self would have been quite pleased knowing the places, people, sights, and cultures that were in his future. I also had the opportunity and good fortune to meet my father during my late twenties and to share some cherished moments with him.*

*Equipped with the support of family, friends, the community, my faith in God, and a university education, I have now been able to reach a previously unimaginable level in my career. My professional career has provided an invaluable opportunity to contribute to the advancement of a number of companies with a vision to positively impact the world. These companies—both small and large in the healthcare field—are actively engaged in improving the lives, health, and wellness of consumers. I know that my younger self would have been astounded by the fact that he would go from running barefoot on an island beach to running meetings in different boardrooms for various corporations.*

*As for questions #2 to # 6 above, at this point, my genuine answer is that only time will tell. It will take a full and complete life in order to answer those thought-provoking questions. The most accurate and unbiased answers will be available at the end of my life, from the people who have been closest to me both on personal and professional basis.*

*The only comment that I can offer is that the things that I value most in life are family, teamwork, truth, courage and integrity. Though more times than I would like to admit, these are the areas which are the most challenging and take the greatest effort to stay true to in my core character. At this stage in life, my greatest desire is to share the knowledge, wisdom and understanding gained so far with today's youth in order to help harness their previously unrecognized and unused talents and skills*

Chapter take-away: As you set out on the path before you there will be many life decisions and choices to make, which will lead you to your ultimate dreams or destinations on your journey. It is important to keep in mind your ultimate desires or goals and to check your progress on a regular annual basis and to revise them as necessary. Taking deliberate care to monitor your overall progress will help to avoid potential disappointment in the future, in which you wake up one day in your fifties and find that your progress is vastly different than the vision you held in your youth.

# The Great Journey of Life

Note - How does your vision for your journey of life compare with your current reality? Are you on the right path?

_____

_____

_____

_____

_____

_____

_____

_____

_____

_____

## Garnet Thompson

# Chapter Two

# Holding On To the Vision

Every person who has ever been born on Earth shares one thing in common. We each have a unique set of talents, gifts or contributions to use or make before our life ends. Whether we discover our purpose for living or not depends on us and how we spend our time. Each person has something special to contribute to society, history, and the people we come in contact with during our limited lifespan. Discovering the vision for our lives has the potential to bring us supreme joy or deep sadness. Once we discover our visions or what we want to accomplish by the end of our lives, it brings meaning and purpose to our lives. Having a clear vision for our lives will determine these twenty aspects in our daily journey.

Hence seeing these aspects with 20/20 vision is paramount to living an intentional, fulfilled life.

(1) Vision determines our futures
(2) Vision determines our attitudes
(3) Vision determines our use of time
(4) Vision determines our character
(5) Vision determines our values
(6) Vision determines our choices
(7) Vision determines our level of persistence
(8) Vision determines our friends
(9) Vision determines our motivations
(10) Vision determines our efforts
(11) Vision determines our priorities
(12) Vision determines our health choices
(13) Vision determines our hobbies
(14) Vision determines our finances
(15) Vision determines our lifestyles
(16) Vision determines our self-control
(17) Vision determines our thirst for knowledge
(18) Vision determines our resourcefulness
(19) Vision determines our experiences
(20) Vision determines our thoughts

One of the biggest challenges and obstacles to our happiness is discovering our gifts and purposes in life and how best to contribute to society. The apparent number of individuals who know their purposes in life at an early age appear to be few in number. The majority of people spend many years in what appears to be an endless and unproductive search for meaning. Though this time may appear to be yielding very little fruit, if any, each and every experience adds to our arsenal and knowledgebase to better equip us along the journey.

Parents typically have enormous visions for their children in which they envision their offspring accomplishing brilliant acts of genius proportions that will shape the future world for generations to come. While the same children or young adults are quite unclear as to their specific talents and how best to apply them in life. The most accurate picture appears to come from individuals or mentors in our lives who have an objective view of our capabilities and can envision how our traits, characteristics, knowledge, and most importantly, talents would best benefit society. Having a mentor or someone whose opinion we value is instrumental in determining our success in life. Often these mentors can see our potential without the curtain of fear, which so often obscures our visions of the future before us.

By holding onto the visions we have for our lives, it will provide us with the strength to endure challenges and tragedies, which are unfortunately part of our human existence.

## _Personal Story_

*A deeply ingrained vision held in my mind and heart, for as long as I could remember during my childhood, was to one day meet my father. It may have taken more than a quarter of a century, or to be exact, 27 years since my birth, but that dream was now about to become quite real. It could not have been scripted any better by the professional screenwriters in Hollywood. The search for my biological father would soon be over.*

*It had only been two short months since my fiancée and I had moved into our new home located in a small town in southern Ontario. The news came in the form of an early morning phone call from an aunt in Florida on Mother's Day (May 11th, 1997). My aunt informed me that she had found my father. She stated that my father was currently in Jamaica and proceeded to give me the phone number. I thanked her for the information and quickly but politely ended the conversation.*

*I sat in disbelief for a few moments before calling my fiancée to share the good news. After taking a few deep breaths, I made the unforgettable telephone call. I asked to speak with [first name] Thompson, and the man on the other end replied: "This is [first name] Thompson."*

*I came straight to the point and said, "My name is Garnet Thompson and I'm your son."*

*I told the gentleman my age, where I was born, and my mother's maiden name. He explained that unfortunately, he was in Jamaica attending his father's funeral, therefore this was not a good time to talk over such important matters. I offered my condolences and expressed sorrow in learning that his father (my grandfather) had passed away. He agreed that based on the information I presented to him, it is possible that I might actually be his son. He asked for my home phone number and promised to call me upon his return to the United States. Without hesitation, I gave him my number and expressed my eagerness to hear from him at the conclusion of his unpleasant duty of burying his father. I excitedly shared the details of the phone call with Nadine and then hurried to call my aunt to repeat the account.*

*As that day was Mother's Day, I made two other important phone calls that morning… one to my grandmother and the other to my mother. This would definitely be a Mother's Day phone call to remember forever. I wished them both a happy Mother's Day and broke the news that I had just spoken to my father!*

Chapter take-away: The strongest visions we hold on to are often first conceived during the days of our youth. It is during this stage of life that our search for meaning, purpose, and how we can contribute to society occupies many of our thoughts. Having trusted family member(s), confidant(s) or mentor(s) with which to share your visions and to reach out to for guidance and / or assistance, will be beneficial in achieving your long-held dreams.

# Holding on To the Vision

Note - Who are your mentor(s)? What compelling vision are you holding on to, which will strengthen you through any tough times ahead?

_____

_____

_____

_____

_____

_____

_____

_____

_____

_____

# Chapter Three

# The Foundation and Pillars of Life

Imagine a Greek temple sturdily constructed out of massive, high-quality stone. The foundation responsible for supporting the entire structure for hundreds or thousands of years to come. The columns painstakingly shaped and placed into precise locations in sufficient numbers to bear the weight of the crowning feature the roof. Then finally the roof, meticulously constructed with guidance and input from many hands, takes shape and is placed atop the mighty pillars. The structure is now ready and beckons passersby to stop and come in to share the activities held within.

Our human lives are similar to such a remarkable Greek structure with the foundation on which our lives firmly (or precariously) resting being our character. The roof which sits atop the pillars and foundation is our "Life."

There are six weight-bearing pillars, which have the precious responsibility of keeping everything on track and standing tall throughout the courses of our lives. The six pillars of life are as follows:

- Destiny - Our purpose on Earth, accomplishments, and impact on this world
- Values - Personal moral code of conduct such as family, truth, and integrity
- Standards - Behaviours and attitudes in keeping with one's vision and purpose
- Belief - Faith to know that something is true without evidence for or against it
- Words - powerful verbal or written elements which shape everything in the world
- Actions - Intentional movements to do something or achieve a desired goal.

## CHARACTER

*Character* is the bedrock and foundation on which our lives are slowly built and shared with the people around us. Our character sets us apart from everyone else; it is the thought-driven moral compass which guides our lives. In essence, it is who we are at our core, regardless if anyone is watching us or not. The decisions we make in private or under extreme circumstances provide a glimpse into our true natures. In order to live a successful life in which we are able to realize all our dreams, we must guard our character as if our life depends on it (*because it does!*).

The greatest threats to our character are the unfiltered thoughts which are continually streaming through our minds. The thoughts which come to our minds need to be filtered to determine which ones are in keeping with our visions and dreams for our lives. Any thoughts upon immediate examination which are contrary to our major purposes must be decisively discarded. All other thoughts are then to be stored as valuable seeds of gold, by which we are able to shape the pillars needed to support our lives. A person of good character will have consciously established the structural pillars (i.e. destiny, values, standards, belief, words, and actions) on which to construct the life they have envisioned and intend to live.

## *Personal Story*

*The person in my life who has contributed the most to shaping my character and values is my grandmother. My grandmother, Mavis Leslie, was born on January 8th, 1927, in Jamaica. Born to parents of different ethnicity and race, my grandmother's complexion resembled that of her father who was of Caucasian descent as opposed to that of her mother who was of African descent. Growing up with my fair-skinned grandmother with her long flowing hair allowed for a deeply ingrained appreciation as a child that regardless of skin colour, everyone was the same inside and was of equal value in society.*

*At the time of my birth, my grandmother, who had previously raised five children (four girls and one boy) of her own, readily accepted the responsibility of taking me in and raising me as her sixth child. Being reared by church-going and God-fearing grandparents who had already been seasoned by life and its challenges provided steady role models for a young boy without a father and mother to emulate. As a child, I learned the importance of telling the truth, keeping my word, and doing the things I said I would do.*

*Integrity and honesty were paramount to my grandparents and any breaches early in development were quickly and lovingly corrected. Furthermore, being respectful and polite to adults was taught on a daily basis in the home to ensure the same behaviour would naturally be exhibited when in the company of other members of the community.*

*During the late 1970s, my grandmother and grandfather made plans to immigrate to Canada to seek out a better life for themselves. However, prior to departing for the land of new promises and opportunity, my grandmother made a decision that I would temporarily remain in Jamaica under the close care of the minister of our church and his family. As it was explained to me at that time, the period was expected to be about one year until they were able to successfully establish new roots in "foreign" (i.e. Canada). At which time they would send for me to join them in the new world.*

*The year living with our minister, his wife, their two daughters, and one of their cousins was an instrumental period in my life which taught me many lessons regarding the kindness of people. The year seemed to speed by and before I knew it, my grandmother (who is known to be a lady of her word) made arrangements for me to join them in Canada. By the age of ten, my grandparents made certain that the six pillars which were to support my life were firmly constructed and put in place.*

Chapter take-away: As you travel through childhood into adulthood various paths or temptations will present themselves for you to choose. It is vitally important that you decide ahead of time that you will stay true to your character and values to avoid potential pitfalls which could and will derail your future. Misguided spur of the moment decisions during days of youth have the potential to change the course of your life forever or to create serious problems that could be avoided.

20/20 VISION DREAMS

# The Foundation and Pillars of Life

Note - What do you believe is your destiny? What are your core values and standards which will support the life you desire to live and safeguard your future?

_____

_____

_____

_____

_____

_____

_____

_____

_____

## Chapter Four

# The Currency of Time

Every person on Earth has been given the same 24 hours in a day. What we become and the dreams we achieve, by the time we take our final breath are the result of two things. The first is how we decide to spend the 24 hours each day, and the second is what we *will* to become.

As we open our eyes, rise from bed each morning, and give praise for another day to spend time with family and friends, we must renew the commitment to our mission and the voyage across the ocean of life.

Time is the one commodity on earth which is inarguably limited and which most people seem to waste a great portion of each and every day. At a certain age in each person's life there comes a moment when you realize for yourself that the old saying "time stands still for no one" is very true. This realization often comes at a time when a close relative, friend or loved one has passed away.

We then have to decide either to allow the loss to permanently halt our own voyages in life or to continue on with the memories of our loved ones and be even more determined to fulfill our missions on the planet. Loss often shakes us out of our prior inexplicable complacency related to our unwise use of time. This often helps to crystallize our thinking and we find our own purposes in life, whether it is a life dedicated to carrying on the vision and legacy of our loved ones, or it suddenly dawns on us that we must find a way to live out our own personal vision and dreams.

The average life expectancy for a person is currently accepted to be approximately 72 years. There are several factors that determine lifespan, which we will refrain from examining but there are many resources dedicated to this topic, however, there is insufficient time *(pun intended)* to tackle those factors in this book. While keeping the worldwide life expectancy in mind, we will do some math together to calculate the equivalent number of minutes available to the average person while alive. Here we go, let's calculate the equivalent potential lifespan in minutes. This exercise is helpful to truly gain an appreciation for how many minutes are available to us and thus to make deliberate use of every precious minute with which we have been gifted.

Potential Lifespan in minutes
- 60 minutes in an hour
- 24 hours in a day
- 365 days in a year
- 60 minutes x 24 hours = 1440 minutes in a day
- 1440 minutes x 365 days = 525,600 minutes in a year
- 525,600 minutes x 72 years = 37,843,200 minutes in an average lifespan  **That is well over 37 million minutes in a lifespan!!!**

In theory, each person has been gifted with about 37 million minutes to accomplish his or her voyage across the great ocean of life. A large number of people are working feverishly each day to become millionaires *(in terms of dollars)* without realizing that they arrived at birth as a millionaire *(in terms of minutes)*. The work human beings seem to have been engaged in since the dawn of time has been trading minutes for dollars.

Ironically, this means we have been trading the most limited and precious resource of time, for money, which is actually replaceable.

Whatever dreams are in your heart and mind are the various ports of call and destinations to be charted on your map across the ocean of life. It is entirely up to you when you depart, where you stop, and how much time you spend deciding where to sail; however, keep in mind that each person has a predetermined amount of time to complete their voyage. Time is the one resource that is always flowing and always being depleted, whether we are awake or asleep. Each and every day we must make a promise to ourselves to make purposeful use of every day.

As Calvin Coolidge, the 30th U.S. President so perfectly stated:

> *"Nothing in the world can take the place of Persistence. Talent will not; nothing is more common than unsuccessful men with talent. Genius will not; unrewarded genius is almost a proverb. Education will not; the world is full of educated derelicts. Persistence and Determination alone are omnipotent. The slogan "Press On" has solved and will always solve the problems of the human race."*

Each day will bring unexpected opportunities and challenges, which will test us at times beyond what we feel we are able to manage. In preparation for these challenges, obstacles, floating debris, storms, jagged rocks rising suddenly and sharply out of what appears to be nowhere, we must decide ahead of time that we can and must find a way to get back on course or to stay on track. During these times you may feel like giving up, turning back or simply stopping the voyage, but keep in mind that every person before you who has previously accomplished their life goals and reached the other side of the ocean had the same thoughts at some point and kept going! It is during these times that it will be important to maintain contact with key members of your support crew. They will remind you, as a friend named Wendell once said to me, that "calm waters have never made for good sailing," and that you are more than capable of getting through the dark nights.

## *Personal Story*

*Everything comes with time. Time heals all wounds. Time waits for no one. Time marches on. Time will tell. These are some of the sayings I have heard as a child. Being raised by my grandmother (Gramma) and grandfather (Dada) allowed for a deeper appreciation of the most valuable commodity on Earth (i.e. time), which I was taught is more valuable than all the gold, diamonds or money in the world.*

*Spending time with someone close to you is often the best gift one person can offer to another individual. I recall many weekend evenings between the ages of twelve and fourteen, staying at home and listening to old gospel records in the basement with my grandparents. This was our time to unwind after a long week at school and work, to rejuvenate our minds and to maintain our connection with each other.*

*The main lesson taught by my grandmother was to treat time with respect and to avoid wasting both mine and other people's time. Whenever we were going to go anywhere, whether to a family function, to a wedding, to church or just for a walk, the expectation was that we would agree on a time to leave and honour that agreement by being ready ahead of time and leaving right on time. The reason, as it was explained to my young mind, was that often unexpected situations arise which must be anticipated and handled to allow for the originally planned departure to happen as promised.*

*As time goes by, I have gained a deeper appreciation for this irreplaceable commodity of time, which marches on relentlessly. I have now found myself teaching my own children the same lessons I was taught as a child. I have also adopted some additional expressions learned later in life to assist with my parenting task. These additional expressions are: "If you are early you are on time, if you are on time you are late, and if you are late that is unacceptable." That being said, I have also made an effort to communicate that we must also take the time to look, listen, feel, and touch the lives of people which cross our paths every day.*

*In my youth, it seemed that the tendency was to try to hurry time along, while now, at almost age fifty, the desire is to take life much slower and to savour each passing moment. It's now time to take the time to use our time more wisely. The following is one of my favourite quotes by the Greek Philosopher Heraclitus, which sums it all up: "No man can ever step in the same river twice, for it is not the same river and he is not the same man."*

Chapter take-away: Time is the single most important asset gifted to each person at birth. Though during our days of youth it may seem that we have all the time in the world to plan for our future life, the fact is, time is steadily marching on and the people and circumstances in our lives are constantly changing. We must remind ourselves on a regular basis to find the right balance between spending time on the things which are important to our youthful selves versus the things which will be more important to our future selves. Making the best use of the majority of the passing minutes, hours, days, weeks, months, and years in purposeful pursuits beneficial to our own aspirations, will position us to live our best life without regrets.

# The Currency of Time

Note - What was the most impactful moment in your life which made you realize that time is your most precious asset?

___

___

___

___

___

___

___

___

___

___

## 20/20 Vision Dreams

# Chapter Five

# The Will to Persist

Human willpower is one of the most energizing and electrifying sources of energy in the universe. A mind that is firmly set on achieving a goal, whether realistic or apparently in the realm of fantasy, is more often than not unbeatable and proven right. Talents, genius, knowledge, and skills are all tremendously important to living a fulfilled life, however, any one or all of those previously listed attributes will be surpassed by sheer willpower and persistence.

If a dream is desired badly enough that an individual intends to focus every ounce of strength and is willing to dedicate every waking hour and/or their entire life to that goal, the odds are in their favour that the dream will one day become very real. Willpower will provide the strength to keep on going one step at a time during the darkest and most desperate times in life. The human ability to harness such vast amounts of power is one of the greatest mysteries in life.

How is it possible for two individuals with similar upbringing and similar backgrounds, when faced with similar challenges, to respond so differently? One individual will give in to adversity and resign to a life that is mediocre, while another individual sees the same challenge as an opportunity to bring great storehouses of talent, genius, skill, knowledge, and willpower to bear to succeed in the face of overwhelming odds. The answer lies in the strength of the desire buried deep in the heart and mind of each individual. The desire itself is either a faint spark barely able to illuminate a tiny lightbulb, or it has nuclear level quantities of electrifying willpower capable of providing energy to the individual, along with anyone else lucky enough to be in the vicinity during that individual's lifetime.

An intriguing aspect of willpower is that it is transferable without using physical wires or cables. The act of witnessing an individual displaying vast amounts of willpower causes bystanders with the right receptive attitudes to ignite the fire in their own desires, which may have been unlit or had gone out some time ago. This transfer of willpower is conducted silently and invisibly and goes unnoticed to the masses. Having access to such willpower is important. However, turning on the vast amounts of unlimited stored potential energy takes a concrete decision and an intention to take massive action.

## *Personal Story*

*Growing up in a home with my grandparents, who in my mind were the hardest working people I had ever and will ever meet in my life, instilled in me a deep conviction that the results one achieves come directly from the effort one puts forth. This conviction was severely put to the test during the years in which I attended university. I was always told from my grandparents, aunts, uncles, and other guiding parental figures in my life that getting an education was the most important thing to focus on in life in order to one day achieve my dreams. Therefore, obtaining my university education became an all-consuming desire, which I intended to accomplish with as much effort as needed, no matter the challenges.*

*As such, when the time came for me to leave high school, the only option present in my young mind was to attend university. Any other option such as attending college, taking a year off to find myself or finding a full-time job never crossed my mind as being right for my situation. So, I proceeded to complete the university applications like all the other young adults in my class. I applied to three of the top universities within commuting distance of our home. I knew that funds were quite limited in our home and that I would need to work to supplement any student loans I would receive and pay for my own education along the way.*

*I did not know how I would pay for my first-year tuition, accommodation at a university, food, books and all the other necessities of a scholastic lifestyle, however, I determined that this was the right path for me to travel and I began to take one step at a time. Fortunately, I qualified for a student loan and a student grant, which assisted with paying for my tuition and textbooks. Based on the available funds, which came from a combination of student loans, working part-time at various restaurant jobs since the age of fourteen, and working every weekend throughout my university years, I was able to achieve my dream of obtaining a Bachelor of Science in Chemistry from McMaster University in Hamilton, Ontario, Canada.*

*During the four years it took to obtain my Honours Bachelor of Science degree, it was necessary to make some really tough choices. I had to alternate between living near the university in a rented room and commuting a great distance from home to attend classes. During the first year of university, I rented and shared an apartment with a work acquaintance and traveled about thirty minutes to school and thirty minutes back to the apartment each day regardless of the weather. In my second year, it was necessary to live at home and commute about one hour to school and one hour back home each day. In my third year, after having worked every day during the previous summer in restaurants, I had saved enough money to be able to rent a room a ten-minute walk from the university. In my fourth and final year, it was again financially necessary to live at home and commute from my hometown to attend classes.*

*The years during which it was necessary to commute from home were the most challenging of all due to weather, traffic, and, at times, sheer exhaustion from attending classes all day and studying late into the evenings and nights at the university science library then driving the hour home. The years in between, when I was fortunate enough to live in the same city as the university, were very much appreciated as they involved one less obstacle to obtaining the sought-after degree.*

*The deep desire in my heart and mind to achieve this all-consuming goal provided all the energy and willpower I needed to persist and travel the seemingly endless number of nights back home on the dark, lonely, country roads and highways in thunderstorms, snow storms, and heavy traffic during those years.*

Chapter take-away: As you grow and face new never-before-experienced challenges, it will be vital at times to remember that deep within your being is a great storehouse of willpower and energy waiting to be used at your own discretion and choice. Access to this vast amount of willpower is unlocked by having a big enough reason for why you desire to achieve whatever audacious goal you have decided to pursue.

# The Will to Persist

Note - Take a moment to reflect and describe a time in your life in which sheer willpower and persistence were used to achieve a positive outcome against overwhelming odds.

_____

_____

_____

_____

_____

_____

_____

_____

_____

# Chapter Six

# The Desire to Explore Uncharted Waters

A close relative (let's call her Yolanda) once said to me, "You can't get to great by staying safe." This single piece of wisdom has the potential to launch you into very deep waters and towards the journey of a lifetime. Often, we sit and ponder which direction to take and which opportunities seem right under the circumstances. It is at this time that we find ourselves going around and around in unending circles, analyzing and reanalyzing multiple options and paths that we think will take us to our dreams. It seems that we are intent to find the safest path with the least amount of risk and the least potential for pain. The fear of making a wrong decision, or *seemingly* wrong decision, often results in analysis paralysis.

The fact is, any decision and any direction will bring new experiences, which will either be a direct or indirect path towards the sought-after dream. After setting out on a path, we will soon find out whether it is the right direction. If we find that we are off course, the need for a slight adjustment or a dramatic change of course will become evident. Time and patience are often all that is needed to travel the ocean of life.

Life sometimes has a way of concealing a fortunate circumstance behind what appears to be an unfortunate circumstance. It is only after some time has passed that we realize the initial solution we had devised ourselves was good, but life all along had something great in store if only we had the patience and wisdom to wait. There are an infinite number of outcomes possible in any given set of circumstances, all of which are unknown in the present moment but will slowly become known with time.

As we push out into uncharted waters, we encounter new, never before experienced obstacles, challenges, and pleasant surprises. Every step forward feels like climbing a mountain in the pitch-black dead of night with only the light of a match to illuminate the path for our feet. Needless to say, this limited vision for such a brief period of time is insufficient to identify the obstacles in our path and to devise any clever schemes to outwit life.

Each person is on a separate journey on the ocean of life. Every wind that blows and every new horizon brings with it moments of fear, trepidation, excitement or, at times, outright dread. Though a person may have been born in what appears to be a safe harbour, we are actually built for sailing the open ocean. As we pass other earthly vessels and at times sail together in armadas for safety, there comes a time when each vessel must set out alone to traverse a stormy heading if we are to reach the destination of our lifetime. We find the strength to keep going and to keep fighting through temporary alliances, by the sharing of resources with friends or family members, by hearing a favourite song and, at times, via a kind word from family members or strangers.

## *Personal Story*

*I remember the circumstances quite well that set in motion a series of life-changing decisions which altered the trajectory and life course of our four-member family unit. The telephone call from a recruiter (aka headhunter) initially seemed routine in nature, like the seemingly hundreds of previous calls with promising potential career opportunities to evaluate.*

*In January 2014, I received a call from a previously unknown recruiter informing me of a career advancement opportunity with a well-known and respected company in the health and wellness field. The role would involve uprooting our children's lives and relocating our core family to another city, albeit still in Ontario. It would mean selling our home and moving hundreds of kilometers away from close family and friends, to a new city where we knew absolutely nobody.*

*I listened intently to the recruiter to gather all the relevant details regarding the role, which sounded like a position that would be a promotion and a long-held dream in my mind. However, the idea of relocating was something that had never even crossed my mind as being a potential route in life.*

*Based on the fact that my spouse was working in a field which she desired at the time and both children were settled in a comfortable routine with school, family occasions, church, and our community, I expressed my gratitude and politely stated that it was not a good fit for our family at this time. I informed Nadine of the conversation and details of the role that evening along with the outcome. We then moved on to attend to our parental duties, such as dinner, homework, and catching up on other events of the day. It was a brief conversation, which seemed to have been the end of the matter.*

*A few weeks later, seemingly out of the blue, Nadine raised the subject again and asked if I was interested in the position. We discussed the potential relocation opportunity along with the impact it would have on our family. We decided that taking on this new challenge would be an interesting adventure and we should go for it. If the position was still open after all this time, it would be a sign from above that this was the right path.*

Chapter take-away: Regardless of what stage you are at in life, whether in your youth or further along into adulthood, sometimes a path in life which you had never crossed your mind suddenly appears before you. You will need to think about it, evaluate the pros and cons, and answer the following question for yourself: should you stay on your pre-charted course or should you take this new uncharted path, which seems to offer a route to your ultimate destination? After you have performed the required amount of diligent analysis, you must decide and go for it! Remember the advice offered from Yolanda, "You can't get to great by staying safe." Sail on and adjust your course accordingly as you experience new never before imagined circumstances.

# The Desire to Explore Uncharted Waters

Note - What major life storm have you most recently experienced and what lesson(s) did you learn after the storm had passed?

_____

_____

_____

_____

_____

_____

_____

_____

_____

## 20/20 VISION DREAMS

# Chapter Seven

# Winds of Adversity

Staying on course takes conscious effort, willpower, and an unyielding intention to fulfill the vision(s) given to each of us. There are times in life when storms are forecast, which allows us to make course adjustments and preparations to tackle these known challenges. However, from time to time unexpected winds of adversity seem to come upon us overnight. Whether it is the loss of a parent or child, the loss of a job or unimaginable challenges encountered during our youth.

The important thing to remember is that unexpected winds of adversity will eventually cross our paths on our journey. The winds in life will range from no wind at all, to a gentle breeze on a warm day, to a short-lived gust of wind on a cold day, all the way to rare hurricane level blasts of sustained winds, which have the power to blow us a great distance off course or to potentially end our journey forever.

These rare once (or twice) in a lifetime hurricane level winds come to test or build our levels of commitment and desire to live our dreams. At these times in life, the choices we make are eye-opening. Knowing ahead of time that the temptation will arise to give up entirely allows us to pre-build support systems (i.e. trusted allies, confidants or our faith in a higher power) in order to successfully navigate these tests in life.

It is during these adversity-filled periods of time that we must consciously recognize them as opportunities to build or use our willpower to get through the storm. Giving up or at worst considering suicide during these times only results in one outcome, which may seem like the only way out, but it is a *permanent* solution to a severe but *temporary* adversity in life. Fully understanding and appreciating this fact will allow for recognition of the next step which can improve on the current undesirable situation.

In such challenging times, a kind word from someone you know or even a complete stranger can make such a difference that they may never know. Reaching out to someone you trust in your "village" can provide a different perspective and identify the right path forward. I don't know you, however I know that you are a blessing here on earth. Whenever you experience a tremendously challenging time in your life, keep fighting because you are stronger than the situation. It is my sincere hope that if you are going through a severely tough situation in your life at this time, that you push through it. Stay strong, and keep moving forward. It's important to help each other with encouragement and kindness. Words cost us nothing but the willingness to offer them to someone. Kind words can make all of the difference in the world. Showing someone love could be the highlight of their day. The words we tell ourselves and others are so important.

Once we push through the curtain of fear, we find our dreams on the other side. Then we realize that the storm is moving and it will eventually pass. This realization brings with it a new level of determination and hope that we have what it takes to tackle the journey. It is at these very moments that our creativity comes alive and we dig deep to harness previously unrecognized and unused talents and skills to grow stronger physically, spiritually, and/or emotionally.

## _Personal Story_

*The sudden and unexpected passing of Nadine's father, my father-in-law Trevor Cooper (aka "TC" to his closest relatives and friends) was one of those rare hurricane level winds which shook our family to the core. TC was a relatively tall man of substantial stature with male pattern baldness. Nadine's father was a hard-working electrician by trade but was a scholar, philosopher, and doctor in his heart and mind. TC passed away within about two weeks of learning that he had cancer.*

*I first met TC some months after Nadine and I began dating. We were invited to a Sunday dinner at his home. Nadine's parents were traditional Jamaican parents and kept strictly to the norms and practices of Caribbean island culture despite living in Canada for over twenty years. We arrived for dinner at the appointed hour and were greeted at the front door with big smiles and warm hugs from both Trevor and Gyda (Nadine's mother).*

*We were then politely ushered into the well-decorated and immaculate living room to begin the evening with conversation before having dinner. After making the initial introductory exchanges including place of residence, level of education, and family history, Nadine and her mother headed towards the kitchen to tend to the pleasant aromas of spice and seasoning now filling the air and wafting into the living room. TC, with a smile on his face, motioned with his hand and said that he would like to speak with me in private on the front porch.*

*After relocating to two lawn chairs, which appeared to have been strategically staged on the front porch, we chatted. After a few minutes of exchanging pleasant comments regarding the pristine condition of my bright red 1993 Nissan 240SX parked directly in front of the family home, the real planned conversation was about to begin. TC, being a practical gentleman, got straight to the point. He asked, "What are your intentions towards my daughter?" Without getting into all the details of the ensuing back and forth dialog for the next hour, suffice it to say that TC was pleased with the answers provided and we re-entered the home to partake in our first of many family meals to come over the years.*

*In a relatively short period of time, TC and I became close friends and he became the father figure and confidant in my life that was missing and genuinely welcomed. During every occasion we met up until his passing, he made a conscious effort to hold a one-on-one dialog with me to inquire how I was doing and what valuable contributions I had made at my place of employment since our last talk. These talks were held in his home, off to the side at another family member's home, at a wedding or while tending to the garden. TC also made it a deliberate practice to share the details of some new medical or scientific knowledge he had recently acquired from his voracious reading habits.*

*During the last two weeks of TC's life, I had the opportunity to witness first hand a man being told that he had less than one week to live. TC displayed enough courage and dignity upon hearing the news to strengthen the nurses, doctors, friends, and family that were with him during his final days. I was present in the hospital room when TC asked the doctor to tell him straight about his prognosis without sugar-coating it. After hearing that he had only a week to live, TC turned to each person in the room and gave us each some final words of wisdom. Amongst the gems he was known to state on other regular occasions were:*

*(1) The greatest thing is to know.*
*(2) The second greatest thing is the word (spoken or written).*
*(3) Plan your work and work your plan.*

*After taking a short nap due to the medication flowing through his system, TC continued with teaching a final lesson. He looked me in the eye and said, "You have your family to take care of and work to get back to, so go back home." Knowing that this was his final wish for me and most likely the last words I would ever hear from his lips, I acknowledged his instructions, said OK, and left the hospital to carry on with my family responsibilities are per those last gems of wisdom.*

Chapter take-away: It is important to remember that life is filled with both beautiful and tragic moments, which can be extremely powerful. We must prepare ourselves in advance to face one of the harshest realities in life, which is the death of a loved one. No matter how much you love someone, there will come a day when you will have to let them go. However, the positive influence, lessons learned, and impact the person had in our lives are intangible assets we can hold on to forever. The most fitting tribute we can offer our lost loved ones is to decide to live up to our fullest potential and to be a positive force for good in someone else's life.

# Winds of Adversity

Note - What unexpected winds of adversity have you faced? Who or what was helpful and offered you hope to overcome the situation(s)?

_____

_____

_____

_____

_____

_____

_____

_____

_____

# Chapter Eight

# Great Sailing Weather

The temperature is just right, the sun is shining, the winds are steadily blowing moderately from behind, and the sky is a brilliant blue with very few clouds. The most satisfying days on our journey are the days when everything is going as planned. This is the time when all of the time spent studying and mastering the skills required for the journey is suddenly paying off.

The right opportunities are coming our way, the right people are coming into our lives, and a sense of peace permeates our entire beings. The seeds of gold, which were planted with care, nurtured diligently, and guarded against harm, are now starting to bear fruit.

Life is at its best, the waters are calm, and many new lands are visible in the distance.

These blissful periods of time can range from days, month, years or even decades for some individuals. A feeling of inspiration and connectedness to the universe becomes so clear and present that you wonder if it was there all along but had previously simply gone unnoticed. Decisions which once seemed challenging and dreadful are now made with relative ease and are filled with tremendous joy and satisfaction. All of the things, people, situations, and happiness from the original vision are experienced with maximum stimulation of all of your five human senses.

The realization hits you that these are the times you had dreamt of all along during tough periods. A sense of gratitude washes over you like a gentle warm wave against a white sandy beach at the end of a day in paradise. It is at this time you understand that the universe is unlimited and willing to provide the deepest desires and wishes of your heart. Everyone in close proximity to you and in your immediate path is benefiting from the long-awaited bounty of riches washing ashore. You are now able to skillfully sail into new ports to meet new and interesting people and experience their cultures.

As you rise each day, you reaffirm to yourself that you're the luckiest and most blessed individual on the planet. You vow to share as much of this new-found wealth as possible with your family, friends, acquaintances, and sometimes even complete strangers. The need to be of service occupies most of your waking hours and you are constantly looking for ways to provide guidance and advice whether solicited or at times unsolicited to other travellers along the way.

## *Personal Story*

*It was now time to graduate from university; four years of challenging and life-altering experiences were drawing to a close. The long-held dream of obtaining an Honours Bachelor of Science Degree in Chemistry from McMaster University would soon be realized. Everything was now going my way!*

*The graduation ceremony was attended by all of the closest individuals in my life at that time, which consisted of my mother, my father-in-law, my brothers, a sister, my grandmother and grandfather along with a few select friends. After graduation, it was now time to seek gainful employment in my field of study.*

*However, until the expected dream job making use of my Honours Chemistry degree was obtained, it was necessary to accept some honest work in the restaurant industry, in which I had several years of experience during my high school career. Prior to leaving school, I had visited the guidance office one last time and had completed and submitted an application for a posted six-month contract position to work as a chemist for a well-known pharmaceutical company in the area.*

*After moving back home that summer, I applied for a position as a sous chef at a Golf & Country Club just outside of town. I was excited about the opportunity since it meant I would be working directly with a real chef. The hiring manager instructed me to report to work the following Monday and to ask for Chef Simon. I went to work for a just single week with Chef Simon and was in awe of the skills he so competently demonstrated in the kitchen. However, fate was knocking on my door and my days working as a sous chef at the Golf & Country Club would be short-lived.*

*I received a call from the Human Resources department at the pharmaceutical company to which I had applied before leaving university. I was asked to come in for an interview the following week. The level of excitement in my mind, body, and heart was more than I had ever experienced in my life. I felt that I was about to take the first step on a journey, which I knew was predestined for my life.*

*I was subsequently offered a six-month contract position for a salary that I thought at the time was an astronomical amount. I recall asking the Human Resources Manager repeatedly if they were actually going to pay me for doing similar testing that I had already performed during my years at school and thoroughly enjoyed. It must have seemed strange to the Human Resources Manager at that time. However, I thought it would be incredible if this was real. I happily worked for the first two weeks and was then* *handed a cheque for $937.50. The fact that this dollar amount remains in my mind until the present day goes to show how much of an impact this experience had on my young mind. Needless to say, I was on cloud nine and it was smooth and clearing sailing for many years to come!*

Chapter take-away: Time, persistence, genuine effort, and the right attitude will undoubtedly bring about the rewards and worldly riches you desire. Life is filled with abundant opportunities and blissful periods, which you deserve. Every day is a new opportunity to take deliberate steps forward to achieve whatever goals you have decided to pursue. When the moment arrives that you fulfill a long-held dream or desire, it will create within you a deep sense of satisfaction and confirmation that the dream was indeed given to you to make it real.

20/20 Vision Dreams

# Great Sailing Weather

Note - Which bliss-filled days and most satisfying experiences on your journey so far comes to mind?

_____

_____

_____

_____

_____

_____

_____

_____

_____

_____

_____

GARNET THOMPSON

# Chapter Nine

# Excess Baggage Overboard

As we sail along through life, we become more skilled at identifying the habits and fears that, when in the right balance, will propel us forward or that, when out of balance, will weigh us down like anchors. Every person has some degree of self-awareness, which is helpful in order to examine our lives and to make the necessary changes to improve our personal and/or professional results.

Some of the habits we hold onto seem to have been programmed into us from birth, while other habits appear to have slowly developed and become part of our beings without us even noticing. Some of the common destructive habits shared by people ever since humans have walked the face of our planet are listed below.

## Twenty Deadly Habits that Will Disrupt Your Journey of Life

(1) Sleeping too much
(2) Eating too much
(3) Drinking too much
(4) Talking too much
(5) Complaining
(6) Procrastinating
(7) Thinking negative thoughts
(8) Overthinking situations
(9) Failing to take action
(10) Doubting our own abilities
(11) Trying to be perfect
(12) Wasting time
(13) Exercising too little
(14) Smoking
(15) Gossiping
(16) Seeking approval from others
(17) Going with the crowd
(18) Being selfish
(19) Working too much
(20) Trying to always be right.

It is helpful to stop for the next hour before continuing on and to rate yourself on a scale of one to ten, on how free you are from the above habits. One being completely free from the destructive habit, ten being completely entangled by the destructive habit. By first making a true assessment, it will then be possible to determine which habits need to be corrected and brought into balance. If you have rated yourself a total score of twenty, you may want to revisit the exercise again in a few days or have someone close to you provide their objective rating to help with the desired self-improvement process.

On the other end of the scale, if you have rated yourself a total of 100 to 200 points, then it may be time take a serious look at the personal and professional results in your life and compare them to the dreams held in your mind as a child. Chances are, your life is completely the opposite to what you had imagined and it is now clear that drastic changes are needed to get back on track. The good news is that by coming to this realization you have taken the first step in the right direction towards achieving your major dreams in life.

The next step is to take a look at the fears in our lives which, when out of balance, have the power to also strand us on a lonely deserted island or to leave us adrift in the open ocean without any support or power to move towards a safe harbour and weather the storms in our lives.

## Ten Deadly Fears Which Can Halt Your Journey in Life

(1) Fear of failure
(2) Fear of success
(3) Fear of death
(4) Fear of fears
(5) Fear of poverty
(6) Fear of criticism
(7) Fear of not being loved
(8) Fear of sickness
(9) Fear of getting old
(10) Fear of rejection.

Once again, it will be helpful to stop reading the book at this time and take the next thirty minutes to truly examine your life so far to determine if any of the above ten fears have influenced the personal and professional outcomes and results in your life. Everybody has dreams and everybody has fears. Chances are that one of the above ten fears looms much larger in your life in different situations. It will often make its unwanted appearance without warning. It will seem quite irrational when examined closely.

When fear begins to rise in your body, first up your legs, then into your stomach, then through your arms, and finally out through your mouth by way of speech, the fear will try to paralyze you and stop your journey. However, by demanding of yourself to have the courage and conviction to face your fears or decide that the dream you once held is not as powerful as you had first thought, the decision will become quite clear as to which steps are next. Fear in the right amount is valuable and helpful to protect us from potential harm or harmful situations. It serves as an early warning system telling us that we are about to take on a challenge for which some additional preparation maybe required. It provides a prompt alerting us of the need for conscious and deliberate focus to ensure we are best positioning ourselves for the desired outcome in situations where the outcome is of importance to us. Will you give up or will you give it all you have and push past the fear? The outcome of the situation which triggered the fear being experienced in your body depends on you making the conscious decision that you will live your dreams no matter what challenges come your way.

Fear—when out of balance—is unwanted baggage and has the power to blind us from the dreams that are directly in front of us. When we look intensely enough, we will often catch a glimpse of the dream and realize that it is time to throw the excess fear overboard and sail on!

A powerful mental exercise to do over the next thirty minutes is described below.

Begin by visualizing thirty open suitcases all lined up in front of you and taking the above twenty deadly habits and ten deadly fears then closing them each in an individual suitcase, then tossing the suitcases one at a time as far as you can overboard to forever sit on the bottom of the ocean.

*(Pause to complete exercise) - The habits and fears are repeated below to assist with the exercise. Pace yourself and have some fun with this activity. Feel free to change your throwing arm and rest as necessary to avoid over overexertion.*

*Ready, set, go!*

## Twenty Deadly Habits that Will Disrupt Your Journey of Life

Sleeping too much
Eating too much
Drinking too much
Talking too much
Complaining

Procrastinating
Thinking negative thoughts
Overthinking situations
Failing to take action
Doubting our own abilities
Trying to be perfect
Wasting time
Exercising too little
Smoking
Gossiping
Seeking approval from others
Going with the crowd
Being selfish
Working too much
Trying to always be right.

## Ten Deadly Fears Which Can Halt Your Journey in Life

Fear of failure
Fear of success
Fear of death
Fear of fears
Fear of poverty
Fear of criticism
Fear of not being loved
Fear of sickness

Fear of getting old
Fear of rejection.

Welcome back! If you have taken the time to truly visualize and complete this powerful mental and moderate physical exercise, as silly as it may have seemed, you should now feel a renewed conviction and a new level of freedom in your mind to pursue all your dreams with much more vigor and power. *(Note - Did you notice which particular habit(s) and/or fear(s) you made the greatest effort to throw as far as possible?)*

Congratulations and thank you for participating in the exercise! We can now be free to sail on unimpeded towards the many ports of call and live new dreams each and every day.

## *Personal Story*

*The personal story I am sharing in this chapter is one of the most challenging ones to write and it was a tough decision to include it in this book in such a public way. As most people who know me can attest, I am by nature a very private person. My tendency towards being a private person may have been due to the circumstances surrounding my childhood. I have never been one to seek the spotlight or to stand out for fear of criticism.*

*I was raised by my grandmother and grandfather from birth. My grandfather has since passed away, but I remain very close with my grandmother. As it so often seems with children raised without their biological mother and father, there is a sense of unworthiness which looms large for long periods of the individual's life. In looking back over the landscape of my life and being honest and transparent, this feeling is the biggest excess baggage that I struggled with as a child and well into my late twenties.*

*I grew up in Jamaica during the 1970s with my grandparents, aunts, uncles, cousins, friends, and close friends of the family, which provided a broad community network of well-meaning parental figures. Looking back now, while writing these words, it is evident that the aunts and uncles in my life appeared to have had some sense of the potential gap in my life and made an extra effort to treat me with the same love and kindness they offered to their own children. To them, I publicly offer my deepest heartfelt gratitude.*

*The impact of growing up as a child while witnessing your half brothers, half sister, cousins and friends living with and being raised by both their biological mothers and fathers was a profound experience. It took almost three decades from my birth until I was able to shake the feelings and thoughts related to a sense of inadequacy.*

*It seems that being able to finally meet my father when I was twenty-seven allowed the grief and trauma from those childhood years to finally be buried in the past.*

*I had the great fortune prior to turning thirty of sitting down with both my biological mother and my biological father. Just the three of us at a table in a restaurant to share our very first and most likely final meal together in our entire lives. It was one of the most profound moments in my life to date.*

*In the moment, it truly felt like I was hovering above the table watching the whole scene unfold and recording it in vivid colour with sound in my memory for future and frequent playback. I still have a souvenir of that lunch meal: it is a toothpick with a Canadian flag on one end. The toothpick was used to hold my sandwich together. I found myself discreetly picking up the toothpick and placing it into my pocket. I suppose at the time I felt that I needed proof that that "family" meal had actually taken place.*

*The simple act of meeting my biological father and being able to see the family resemblance and to finally feel a sense of acceptance and belonging filled the gap in my heart which appeared to have been unknown to myself and existed since birth. A sense of peace and tranquility replaced the spot in my mind where unworthiness and anger had secretly taken up residence in my life for so long.*

*Once this unwanted excess baggage was tossed overboard with both hands and using all my might, it was now time to sail on into life as an adult. It was now clear to me that now that that chapter from my youth was closed, all the other dreams which were being compiled in a list for my life would be possible. Since the previously thought impossible family reunion had become possible, then it stood to reason that everything else was now possible.*

Chapter take-away: It is important from time to time to stop and examine our lives to determine which habit(s) and fear(s) are working against our desired outcomes. By taking deliberate and decisive action to eliminate those habit(s) and push through the fear(s) you will experience a renewed sense of hope. We must then demand of ourselves the courage to face all fear-inducing circumstances on the path to our dreams if we are to live our best and most fulfilling lives.

# Excess Baggage Overboard

Note – *Which particular habit(s) and/or fear(s) did you make the greatest effort to throw as far as possible?*

_____

_____

_____

_____

_____

_____

_____

_____

_____

_____

_____

# Chapter Ten

# Crossing Paths with Special Voyagers

Along our path in life, we sometimes come across some special people and we feel a deep connection to them and a sense of responsibility to protect them. These special voyagers, if we are fortunate enough to have come into our lives and are able to spend some time with them, will bring us more joy and happiness than we could ever give back to them.

Whether these people come into our lives for decades, years, months, days, hours or mere minutes, we know them immediately when we meet them. Our memories of such individuals will spring to mind in certain circumstances when a reminder of the lessons that they taught us is once again needed. These lessons vary and are often simple but very powerful such as the following:

(1) Be patient
(2) Be kind
(3) Be happy
(4) Be thankful
(5) Be forgiving
(6) Be good
(7) Be considerate
(8) Be loving
(9) Be faithful
(10) Be gentle
(11) Be joyful
(12) Be strong.

## *Personal Story*

*I met one of these special voyagers when I first began my professional career after graduating from university. Out of respect for the privacy of this individual who has since passed away, we will call her "Joy" to represent the intangible but precious benefit and impact she brought into the lives of the people she met. I had the good fortune to know this voyager, Joy, for about two decades. We had worked together for many years over different intervals at various companies. Strangely enough, my memories of Joy have very little to do with our professional accomplishments over the years but are mostly related to the many lessons she either consciously or unconsciously deposited in my life forever.*

*It was spring 2013 when I heard some troubling news that Joy was recently and unexpectedly out of work. After reaching out directly to Joy to check on her and to provide some encouragement, the message received back was that she was staying positive and appreciated the support she was receiving from her family and friends. Over the many years we worked together, a talent which Joy had often shared with her co-workers and friends was her culinary skills, especially her baking skills. Joy's European upbringing and background had been instrumental in her developing and mastering the art of creating sweet and savoury baked delights, which tantalized every pallet lucky enough to experience her tasty morsels.*

*A week after I had contacted Joy, she sent a text message with her new home address and an offer for me to bring my family by anytime for a visit. This now feels like a lost opportunity and a weak excuse, but at the time the hustle and bustle of home life, work life, and all of the various commitments made it a challenge to accept this genuine offer to spend time together. Years later, I realized despite having visited Joy on a number of other occasions in her home and meeting her at the homes of other friends, these offers to share time and to partake in her baked goods would one day end. Although we didn't meet at that time to share in Joy's baked delicacies, we continued to correspond somewhat regularly using text messages. These texts date back about five years and remain on my cell phone to the present day.*

*Over the next few weeks, our circle of long-time friends was shaken by the news that a co-worker and friend (let's call her Flo) was critically ill and not expected to recover. Joy informed me that she spent her newfound free time keeping busy by visiting Flo, painting, and socializing. Joy visited our ailing friend Flo quite often over the following weeks until Flo passed away in July of that same year. Joy and Flo had a special bond in each other's lives; they were best friends and often took vacations together multiple times each year to different tropical islands.*

*I received a text from Joy at 3:56 a.m. on Friday, July 19th stating that Flo had passed away and she thought she should let me know. Strange as it may seem, we corresponded back and forth in the early of hours of the morning via text. Looking back on our written communication, it seemed to have been an easier method to communicate without causing further mental anguish until we could speak in person. The texts chronicle Joy's report of Flo having gotten worse and subsequently collapsing. We communicated how much fun we had with Flo and how she would be missed. Joy stated that she lost a good friend and had fond memories of Flo, herself, and myself interacting at work. My last text that morning at 5:17 a.m. reads, "I remember, that was fun."*

*Whenever my mind turns to Joy, I look back on these and other numerous texts which now serve as a time capsule and a priceless treasure of her positive words freely offered to myself during her deepest and darkest times before she herself passed away. Sadly, but fortunately enough for us, during Joy's final months, Nadine, Jasmine, Anthony, and I did have an opportunity to accept what would be the final invitation from Joy to visit her home to spend some time together and to share a meal at her dining table. The lessons learned from this special voyager serve as powerful reminders along the path we travel, while we strive to live out the dreams in our heart. We must remember to make a conscious effort to take the time to touch another voyager's heart along the way.*

Chapter take-away: While on our journey through life, the natural human tendency is to focus on what we want and what is going on in our own lives. When we stop for a few moments on a regular basis to look around at the people in our lives, it will be obvious who are those special people which have come into our lives to teach us important lessons. The truly valuable experiences in lives are those which you find spring to mind under certain circumstances without your conscious effort. By examining those memories, you will find the lesson deposited by a special person to be applied to a situation you are facing at that moment.

# Crossing Paths with Special Voyagers

Note - Who are the special voyager(s) in your life and what lessons have you learned from your time with them?

_____

_____

_____

_____

_____

_____

_____

_____

_____

## Chapter Eleven

# All Hands On Deck

Situations in life will often require many hands or minds to come together and work in a coordinated way in order to arrive at the desired outcome. A key aspect of life—if not the main aspect of life—is building successful relationships. Relationships are vital to the accomplishment of most, if not all, goals or dreams worth pursuing. The focus over the years in society during early childhood education has been reading, writing, and arithmetic. Rightfully so, these are indeed of tremendous importance during any decade or era to come, however, adding relationships as a fourth core subject to the educational curriculum would provide a better understanding of its criticality to human society.

Typically, we first learn to relate to the world around us through our immediate relatives (mother, father, siblings) as the core family structure. As we grow and interact with other individuals in our circle within the community or communities during the course of our lives, we add many additional and widening concentric circles about us. Each subsequent layer of circles or degrees of relationships have a specific purpose and reason in our lives. Although we are at the center of our own relational graph, we are by no means the center of importance. The most important component or features are the interactions going inward and outward from the concentric circles as we live our daily lives.

The interactions themselves and how well they are executed make all the difference in the world towards the results we achieve and the dreams and goals we will eventually accomplish or experience.

## Personal Story

*As the saying goes, "It takes a village to raise a child." A proposed saying which I will take the liberty to offer from the opposite perspective is that, "A child counts on a village to raise him/her." The wisdom held in sayings is quite profound and is eternally true. I suppose that is the reason these nuggets of wisdom have become embedded in the fabric of society whether intentionally or unintentionally and are passed from generation to generation.*

*One of the most challenging yet rewarding and treasured aspects in my life has been having children. Though, if you would have asked me in my mid-twenties the answer would have been, "I'm never having children!" It would probably take a whole other chapter to understand where this feeling and attitude first developed, but suffice it to say growing up in a large extended family with many cousins, brothers, and sisters provided many opportunities to interact with children at varied ages and stages of development, which my younger self seemed to have found quite exasperating.*

*At the time of writing this book, Nadine and I have two children, or more appropriately two young adults. It has definitely taken our "village," consisting of grandparents, parents, aunts, uncles, cousins, brothers, sisters, friends, church members, babysitters, godmothers, godfathers, school teachers, nurses, doctors, librarians, soccer coaches, Pastors, swimming instructors, piano teachers, co-workers, and at times random strangers to get our two young adults to this stage in their lives.*

*The number of personal interactions shared by Jasmine and Anthony with our "village" members over the years are innumerable and priceless. It is incredible to even attempt to think about all the occasions known to us and unknown to us, which have helped to shape their young lives. All of these interactions have left deep traces and an everlasting impact (mostly positive) on their young minds and hearts.*

*We have found that it is at times necessary to share with family and friends both the positive and challenging situations experienced while rearing our children over the years, in order to benefit from the wisdom and support of the community. A key support in their lives has been during overnight visits and sleepovers at the home of their Auntie Janice, Uncle Kendall, and Cousins Zoe, Ava, Sage, and Kai. These occasions have offered many moments for the extended family to celebrate wins by each member since the last get-together, to share advice on how to handle current challenges, and best of all, to share some great food and some laughs in whatever spontaneous activity that sprang to mind.*

*After having moved away from our extended family, these occasions are now reserved for the holidays and special occasions during the year. These are the times when the family holds hands prior to partaking in a spectacular array of home-cooked foods and give thanks for the many blessings in our lives. Each family member is given an opportunity to state in one or two words what they are most appreciative for in their lives. The responses from each individual ranging in age from the youngest toddler capable of speech all the way to treasured village elders in their nineties are thoughtfully absorbed and validated by all gathered by raising our joint hands in the air and cheering. After which a prayer is offered over the meal and the feasting commences.*

Chapter take-away: The family members, friends, classmates, teachers, and strangers who cross our paths on a daily basis provide us opportunities to develop our skill of building human relationships. The community in which we live our lives serves as a support system available for us to reach out to be strengthened and to strengthen others as the need arises. Having a genuine interest in other people will be helpful in maintaining the right attitude necessary to discern what each individual needs during challenging interactions. Taking time and making a conscious effort to improve our skill with human relationships will be key to realizing our dreams.

# All Hands On Deck

Note - Who are the trusted individual(s) in your "village" that you can reach out to for help in a time of need?

# 20/20 VISION DREAMS

# Chapter Twelve

# Treasure Chest of Lessons Learned

While navigating the ocean of life on the journey towards the harbours of our dreams, we can expect to find and collect nuggets of wisdom along the way. I have found that the discovered nuggets of treasured wisdom which have served my life the best have come from the very first thoughts running through my mind immediately upon waking in the mornings. These initial thoughts are quite elusive and most often go by unnoticed and are rapidly replaced with all the cares of the day and the many items which automatically reload from our to do lists.

It has taken many years to notice and arrive at the conclusion that these first thoughts residing on the border as we transition from being asleep to being awake, provide deep and profound guidance for problems and situations we have been struggling with over the past days, weeks, months, and sometimes years. These flashes of insight, if acted upon, have always resulted in a positive outcome to whatever situations were in scope. The origin of these thoughts and insights may forever remain unknown to us, but they are immensely valuable once we train our conscious mind to take notice of them and to take quick and deliberate action to capture them in as much detail as possible.

Examples of these border sleep state thoughts are the following short stories presented in this chapter. As well as the quote on the front cover of this book: "Once we push through the curtain of fear, we find our dreams on the other side." Upon waking one morning many years ago prior to even having the thought to author this book, I found those words running through my mind. I had no idea that this quote would be documented in a book years in the future. It would seem that my mind wandered far into the distant future, retrieved the quote from a book yet to be written, returned to the present time, and deposited the quote written by my future self, like a seed from which this book has grown.

One still elusive dream from my youth is to experience time travel. It is difficult to think and accept that this may have been the case. However, being the dream-seeking, goal-achieving individual I am, I will take this one as a win and check it off the goal list as the time travel dream achieved.

I wrote the following short stories, which came to my mind while writing this book, and I have since shared them on a professional social network platform with other individuals in my field. The key points and nuggets of wisdom stated at the end of each short story are important for the development and maintenance of the right mindset necessary to realize our dreams. It truly is all about perspective, attitude, trust, and integrity. I hope you enjoy the below short stories and find them to be valuable.

## **Two Bricklayers and the Student**

One day on a jobsite there were two bricklayers and there was a student assigned to work with the bricklayers. The student went up to the first bricklayer and said, "What are you doing?"

The bricklayer said, "Kid, I gotta come to this jobsite every day and I gotta stack these bricks. There are thousands of bricks and I gotta stack them one after the other. It's back-breaking, hot, time-consuming work, and I'm working to build this *wall*."

By lunchtime, the student was pretty discouraged and sat down beside the second bricklayer and asked, "Why do you do what you're doing?"

The second bricklayer paused for a moment and said, "I get to come to this jobsite every day and I am placing these bricks in their precise locations, one after the other, and I'm working to build this *school*, where thousands of kids are going to come over the years to learn, to grow, to develop, to go out into the world to live their dreams and I get to be part of that!"

*

I find this story powerful! I have shared it with my teams many times over the years in Good Manufacturing Practices (GMP) training sessions and during team meetings. It helps during communication with our valued plant team members to emphasize that all roles are important and contribute to the overall mission of our company.

It's all about perspective!

## **Two Door-to-Door Salespeople
adapted from Jim Rohn**

One cold and stormy winter morning two door-to-door salespeople living in the same town woke up and peeked through their snow-covered bedroom windows. The wind was blowing, the snow was falling fast, and everything in sight was covered in a deep, heavy blanket of wet snow.

The first salesperson said out aloud, "They can't possibly expect me to go out and make door-to- door sales in weather like this!" Then got back into the warm bed, covered up from head to toe, and went back to sleep.

At the same time, the second salesperson, looking out the bedroom window, seeing the same weather, paused for a second and thought, "Hmm, it's the perfect day to go out and make door-to-door sales. Everybody will be at home, including all the other salespeople."

Then he jumped into the shower, got dressed, and headed out the door. The day resulted in an opportunity to meet new customers and a new company record number of daily sales.

\*

I find this story to be a powerful reminder! I have shared it with team members in a Good Manufacturing Practices (GMP) training session in the past. It is extremely effective in demonstrating that the results we achieve are dependent on us having the right perspective along with maintaining the right attitude.

It's all about attitude!

## **The Auditor, the Audit Host, and a Speeding Bus**

One day, while on a walking tour between buildings to conduct a foreign regulatory GMP inspection, an auditor and an audit host came to a busy intersection with traffic lights. The pair, having just recently met, casually chatted and waited for the signal to cross the street. Once the walk signal appeared both individuals looked to the left, then looked to the right before deciding to proceed.

As the auditor stepped off the curb, the audit host glanced to the right and noticed a bus approaching the intersection coming directly towards the auditor. The host reached forward with both hands firmly around the auditor's upper body and pulled the auditor out of the path of the bus and back onto the curb.

As the bus sped pass, both individuals stood completely still and looked at each other silently while taking in the near miss. After a few seconds, which seemed like minutes, the highly trained auditor broke the silence and said in a matter-of-fact way, "Well, that was an international incident averted." The pair smiled and laughed with each other.

The host replied: "Yes, that would have made for an interesting audit outcome."

With a high level of trust now unexpectedly and instantly built, the pair continued with the audit and never mentioned the incident again. The incident accelerated the process of building trust and a working rapport, which allowed for the audit to be completed in a transparent, efficient, and effective way.

*

I find this true story very interesting! It helps to demonstrate that trust is the bedrock and foundation of all our human relationships. Once trust is established, whether quickly or slowly built over time by genuine means, everything else will follow.

It's all about trust!

## **Two Law Enforcement Agents and the Quality Manager**

One day, while a Quality Manager was working in the office, the telephone rang as it so often does in such a role. The voice on the other end identified himself as being from law enforcement. It was a call that the intrepid young Quality Manager never expected to receive in a lifetime, except maybe in the movies.

The Quality Manager listened intently as the law enforcement agent posed several questions and provided details regarding the reason for the unexpected call. The agent was interested in speaking with the Quality Manager who was identified as a potential witness with valuable evidence to offer in a case of fraudulent test data being investigated.

A well-intentioned offer was made by the law enforcement agent to meet at the Quality Manager's place of employment. Needless to say, the Quality Manager thought there would be no easy way to explain the occurrence of such a meeting in the workplace, and instead made a counteroffer to meet at a nearby precinct. It was agreed by both parties that it would be more appropriate to meet outside the workplace to avoid any potential misunderstanding of the visit.

Upon arriving at the precinct, it was like a scene straight out the movies. The Quality Manager was quietly ushered into a small rectangular room by two law enforcement agents (a local agent and believe it or not a federal agent). The three individuals sat down at a table with a tape recorder and a stack of files at the center. It appeared that a long line of questioning was about to commence.

The friendly visit ended after several hours, with the law enforcement agents thanking the Quality Manager for taking the time to provide transparent and detailed responses. Business cards were exchanged and the trio parted company that day never to meet again. The Quality Manager returned to work the next day, with a previously established and long-held conviction to do the right thing firmly reinforced.

*

I find this story to be a good reminder. It demonstrates the importance of strict adherence to policies and procedures while completing all duties in our areas of responsibility. It is sometimes helpful to ask ourselves one final question before taking action: "What is the right thing to do?"

It's all about integrity!

Chapter take-away: As you awaken each new day take a moment to notice the first thoughts running through your mind and examine them closely to determine if they offer insight into a challenge or situation you have been thinking about before going to bed the previous night. By training yourself to grasp these elusive first thoughts you will gather insights and wisdom which were routinely unavailable during your busy activity filled days. Taking action to implement these thoughts and ideas will undoubtedly lead you one step closer to a deeply held desire.

# Treasure Chest of Lessons Learned

Note - What are some treasured nuggets of wisdom you have collected so far on your journey in life?

___

___

___

___

___

___

___

___

___

___

# Chapter Thirteen

# The Science of Dreaming

Let's take an overview look at some of the scientific facts and explanations about dreams. Understanding some of the science is important in order to make the best use of the significant amount of time we typically spend during our lifespan on this mostly involuntary and uncontrolled activity. If you, as the reader, would like to obtain a deeper and much richer appreciation of the various scientific theories and research about dreaming, it would be best to consult the many books previously published on this subject.

According to the National Sleep Foundation ([www.sleepfoundation.org](www.sleepfoundation.org)) the following discussions and explanations of dreams are being shared. Quoted excerpts will be presented below to offer you a full undiluted and unchanged explanation as provided by the referenced source.

"In ancient societies, dreams guided political, social and everyday decisions. Early books, including the Bible, are filled with references to divine visions during sleep. On the other hand, Greek philosophers attributed dream content to natural sources, which were precursors of modern theories of dream formation and significance.

In the 19th century, Sigmund Freud promoted one popular theory that dreams gave us access to our unconscious repressed conflicts. He called them "the royal road to a knowledge on the part of the unconscious plays in mental life." However, another early psychoanalyst, Alfred Adler, believed that dreams reflect current lifestyle and offer solutions to contemporary problems.

Interest in modern dream research was revived at the same time as the discovery of rapid eye movement (REM) sleep and its association with an increased frequency in dreaming by Eugene Aserinsky and Nathaniel Kleitman in 1953. "When we look at the importance of dream research we get back to the question 'Does sleep itself have a function?' We know today, if you sleep you have an improved waking experience. We also know that sleep allows dreaming to occur," according to Jim Pagel, MD, director of the Sleep Disorders Center of Southern Colorado and a participating NSF Community Sleep Awareness Partner®. "If dreaming has an actual function, it really supports why we spend a third of our lives sleeping."

While scientists still do not know much about why or how we dream, some have suggested that we typically spend more than two hours dreaming each night. Many people experience their most vivid dreams during REM sleep; less vivid dreams occur at other times of the night. Comparative research has shown that while most mammals and birds show signs of REM sleep, reptiles and other cold-blooded animals scientists still don't know—and probably never will—if animals dream during REM sleep, as humans do. "How can you prove that another person has dreams?" says Jerome Siegel, PhD, a professor of Psychiatry at the UCLA Center for Sleep Research. "You ask them.""

"Dreaming occurs about 90 minutes after falling asleep and increases over the latter part of the night; necessary for providing energy to the brain and body;

brain is active and dreams occur as eyes dart back and forth; bodies become immobile and relaxed; muscles shut down; breathing and heart rate may become irregular; important to daytime performance and may contribute to memory consolidation – but with sleep apnea, some of the benefits of this important sleep stage is lost."

Whether you remember them or not, dreams are a normal part of sleep. Everyone dreams for a total of about two hours per night and dreams can occur during any stage of sleep, although they're most vivid during the REM phase. If you've ever woken up from a happy dream feeling relaxed and rested—or a scary one feeling on edge—you might have wondered whether the content of your shut-eye reveries can make a difference in your overall sleep quality. Here's what's really going on:

## Scary Dreams Linger into the Next Day

Dreams can be positive or negative, and there's no question that <u>nightmares</u> have ramifications that last even after you wake up. Falling back asleep after awakening from a nightmare is tough, and those scary images can affect your mood and behavior the next day, causing the equivalent of a bad-dream hangover.

## Dreams Don't Change Sleep Structure

Despite how it may feel, though, disturbing dreams don't always have a significant effect on your sleep architecture, meaning they won't necessarily change how much time you spend in the different stages of sleep or the number of times you awaken. What they can change: How long it takes to fall asleep at night and how challenging it is for your body to switch between non-REM and REM stages of sleep, which may leave you feeling less rested.

## Does Good Sleep Equal Happy Dreams?

The relationship between dream quality and sleep quality could be likened to the old chicken-and-egg scenario: No one is sure which comes first. Research shows that good sleepers often describe their dreams as being more pleasant and joyful, while people who suffer from insomnia tend to have fewer positive emotions associated with their dreams, but whether or not a happy or sad dream means you'll sleep better or worse still isn't clear.

## Dreams Reflect Reality

Dream content often relates back to what's happening in your waking life. If you're experiencing low stress and plenty of satisfaction in your day-to-day life, you may have more positive dreams. By contrast, if you're depressed or anxious during the day, you may have more unpleasant dreams and compromised sleep quality at night.

The good news is that while you cannot control your dreams directly, you can work on improving your state of mind during the day. This, in turn, may help improve the quality of your dreams—and perhaps sleep—at night."

Chapter take-away: As can be seen from our relatively short exploration into the science of dreaming, the exact source or, mechanism for and more importantly the purpose for being able to dream remains unknown. One thing is certain, dreams—whether while we are asleep or awake during daydreaming episodes—offer us a glimpse into what is possible in our future with a decision, along with hard work, persistence, and determination.

## The Science of Dreaming

Note - What recurring dreams have you experienced during your childhood?

# Chapter Fourteen

# The End of the Voyage

Each day we are able to rise out of bed provides us with another valuable opportunity to evaluate our progress to date and determine if we are truly on track towards living the life of our dreams. Every new day provides us yet another chance to plan or take deliberate steps in the right directions. As we advance in the directions of our deepest desires, it is important to look around at the other travellers in our lives who are on their own dream journeys.

Take a moment to consider all the human beings closest to you in personal relationships and make a life-long commitment to providing them with daily words of encouragement as they walk the paths they are on. Often people are silently seeking a kind word or a sense that someone is in their corner. This sense of support, though intangible, is often the final and most important ingredient or piece of the puzzle that propels an individual onto dizzying new heights.

One of the best ways to position ourselves for success and happiness is to assist others. Our words of encouragement alone could keep them moving in the right direction. The words we speak are the most powerful influence we can offer another human being. Though our words cost us only the time, effort, and willingness to freely offer them to other individuals, they are usually prized intangible assets to the ears of the receiver. The words we deliberately or accidentally deposit into the minds of people who are passively or actively striving towards their dreams can either supercharge their efforts or discourage them to the point of giving up and losing all hope.

At the end of this book are the most valuable pages. It is a section being offered to you to note and track progress on achieving all the desires of your heart. Take some time on a regular basis to think about, capture, and track all the small, medium, large, and enormous dreams which you have entertained in your mind over the years.

What will the end of the journey be like? Will I have made the most out of life? Will I have accomplished anything meaningful? Will I have fulfilled the most important dreams and desires in my heart and my mind? Only time will tell. We each have small dreams, medium dreams, big dreams, and then there are those enormous dreams, which often scare our ourselves and give us goosebumps. Although it is important to share some of our dreams with a trusted confidant, it is wise to keep the oversized giant dreams private.

One of the lessons life has taught me over the years is that not everyone will share your enthusiasm for those massive dreams. Well-meaning family members and friends will seek to provide advice and counselling that, if you allowed it, would keep you from taking another step forward towards the attainment of those giant desires. It is often best to keep such monstrous desires private and work steadily, deliberately, and slowly without any mention of them to a single soul. Once we have brought them to reality, they will speak loudly for themselves and astonish the people in our lives as well as ourselves.

I sincerely hope that this book has been useful for you at whatever stage you find yourself on your journey across the ocean of life. At this time, you may feel uncertain about the direction for your life or perhaps you may have been told there's only one way to go. Whether you are on the cusp of graduating from high school, university or on the verge of another significant life change, I trust that you will benefit from this interactive experience. May all your dreams become a reality one day. Let's make them happen by daring to dream. Thank you for taking the time to read this book. Cheers!

# The End of the Voyage

Note - What enormous dream(s) for your life do you have which scares you and gives you goosebumps?

_____

_____

_____

_____

_____

_____

_____

_____

_____

_____

_____

# YOUR List of 100 Dreams

List of 100 Dreams Tracker

Using the S.M.A.R.T goals method – Specific, Measurable, Achievable, Results-Focused, Timed

| # 1 | What: |
|---|---|
| | How: |
| | Why: |
| | When: |
| | Status: |
| | Completed Reality Date: |
| # 2 | What: |
| | How: |
| | Why: |
| | When: |
| | Status: |
| | Completed Reality Date: |

| # 3 | What: |
| | How: |
| | Why: |
| | When: |
| | Status: |
| | Completed Reality Date: |
| # 4 | What: |
| | How: |
| | Why: |
| | When: |
| | Status: |
| | Completed Reality Date: |
| # 5 | What: |
| | How: |
| | Why: |
| | When: |
| | Status: |
| | Completed Reality Date: |

## 20/20 VISION DREAMS

| # 6 | What: |
| --- | --- |
| | How: |
| | Why: |
| | When: |
| | Status: |
| | Completed Reality Date: |
| # 7 | What: |
| | How: |
| | Why: |
| | When: |
| | Status: |
| | Completed Reality Date: |
| # 8 | What: |
| | How: |
| | Why: |
| | When: |
| | Status: |
| | Completed Reality Date: |

| # 9  | What: |
|      | How: |
|      | Why: |
|      | When: |
|      | Status: |
|      | Completed Reality Date: |
| # 10 | What: |
|      | How: |
|      | Why: |
|      | When: |
|      | Status: |
|      | Completed Reality Date: |
| # 11 | What: |
|      | How: |
|      | Why: |
|      | When: |
|      | Status: |
|      | Completed Reality Date: |

# 20/20 Vision Dreams

| # 12 | What: |
| | How: |
| | Why: |
| | When: |
| | Status: |
| | Completed Reality Date: |
| # 13 | What: |
| | How: |
| | Why: |
| | When: |
| | Status: |
| | Completed Reality Date: |
| # 14 | What: |
| | How: |
| | Why: |
| | When: |
| | Status: |
| | Completed Reality Date: |

| # 15 | What: |
|  | How: |
|  | Why: |
|  | When: |
|  | Status: |
|  | Completed Reality Date: |
| # 16 | What: |
|  | How: |
|  | Why: |
|  | When: |
|  | Status: |
|  | Completed Reality Date: |
| # 17 | What: |
|  | How: |
|  | Why: |
|  | When: |
|  | Status: |
|  | Completed Reality Date: |

| # 18 | What: |
|      | How: |
|      | Why: |
|      | When: |
|      | Status: |
|      | Completed Reality Date: |
| # 19 | What: |
|      | How: |
|      | Why: |
|      | When: |
|      | Status: |
|      | Completed Reality Date: |
| # 20 | What: |
|      | How: |
|      | Why: |
|      | When: |
|      | Status: |
|      | Completed Reality Date: |

| | |
|---|---|
| # 21 | What: |
| | How: |
| | Why: |
| | When: |
| | Status: |
| | Completed Reality Date: |
| # 22 | What: |
| | How: |
| | Why: |
| | When: |
| | Status: |
| | Completed Reality Date: |
| # 23 | What: |
| | How: |
| | Why: |
| | When: |
| | Status: |
| | Completed Reality Date: |

| # 24 | What: |
| | How: |
| | Why: |
| | When: |
| | Status: |
| | Completed Reality Date: |
| # 25 | What: |
| | How: |
| | Why: |
| | When: |
| | Status: |
| | Completed Reality Date: |
| # 26 | What: |
| | How: |
| | Why: |
| | When: |
| | Status: |
| | Completed Reality Date: |

| # 27 | What: |
|---|---|
| | How: |
| | Why: |
| | When: |
| | Status: |
| | Completed Reality Date: |
| # 28 | What: |
| | How: |
| | Why: |
| | When: |
| | Status: |
| | Completed Reality Date: |
| # 29 | What: |
| | How: |
| | Why: |
| | When: |
| | Status: |
| | Completed Reality Date: |

## 20/20 Vision Dreams

| # 30 | What: |
|---|---|
| | How: |
| | Why: |
| | When: |
| | Status: |
| | Completed Reality Date: |
| # 31 | What: |
| | How: |
| | Why: |
| | When: |
| | Status: |
| | Completed Reality Date: |
| # 32 | What: |
| | How: |
| | Why: |
| | When: |
| | Status: |
| | Completed Reality Date: |

| # 33 | What: |
|---|---|
|  | How: |
|  | Why: |
|  | When: |
|  | Status: |
|  | Completed Reality Date: |
| # 34 | What: |
|  | How: |
|  | Why: |
|  | When: |
|  | Status: |
|  | Completed Reality Date: |
| # 35 | What: |
|  | How: |
|  | Why: |
|  | When: |
|  | Status: |
|  | Completed Reality Date: |

## 20/20 Vision Dreams

| # 36 | What: |
| --- | --- |
| | How: |
| | Why: |
| | When: |
| | Status: |
| | Completed Reality Date: |
| # 37 | What: |
| | How: |
| | Why: |
| | When: |
| | Status: |
| | Completed Reality Date: |
| # 38 | What: |
| | How: |
| | Why: |
| | When: |
| | Status: |
| | Completed Reality Date: |

| # 39 | What: |
|      | How: |
|      | Why: |
|      | When: |
|      | Status: |
|      | Completed Reality Date: |
| # 40 | What: |
|      | How: |
|      | Why: |
|      | When: |
|      | Status: |
|      | Completed Reality Date: |
| # 41 | What: |
|      | How: |
|      | Why: |
|      | When: |
|      | Status: |
|      | Completed Reality Date: |

## 20/20 Vision Dreams

| # 42 | What: |
| --- | --- |
| | How: |
| | Why: |
| | When: |
| | Status: |
| | Completed Reality Date: |
| # 43 | What: |
| | How: |
| | Why: |
| | When: |
| | Status: |
| | Completed Reality Date: |
| # 44 | What: |
| | How: |
| | Why: |
| | When: |
| | Status: |
| | Completed Reality Date: |

| # 45 | What: |
| | How: |
| | Why: |
| | When: |
| | Status: |
| | Completed Reality Date: |
| # 46 | What: |
| | How: |
| | Why: |
| | When: |
| | Status: |
| | Completed Reality Date: |
| # 47 | What: |
| | How: |
| | Why: |
| | When: |
| | Status: |
| | Completed Reality Date: |

# 20/20 Vision Dreams

| # 48 | What: |
|---|---|
| | How: |
| | Why: |
| | When: |
| | Status: |
| | Completed Reality Date: |
| # 49 | What: |
| | How: |
| | Why: |
| | When: |
| | Status: |
| | Completed Reality Date: |
| # 50 | What: |
| | How: |
| | Why: |
| | When: |
| | Status: |
| | Completed Reality Date: |

| # 51 | What: |
| | How: |
| | Why: |
| | When: |
| | Status: |
| | Completed Reality Date: |
| # 52 | What: |
| | How: |
| | Why: |
| | When: |
| | Status: |
| | Completed Reality Date: |
| # 53 | What: |
| | How: |
| | Why: |
| | When: |
| | Status: |
| | Completed Reality Date: |

## 20/20 VISION DREAMS

| # 54 | What: |
|---|---|
| | How: |
| | Why: |
| | When: |
| | Status: |
| | Completed Reality Date: |
| # 55 | What: |
| | How: |
| | Why: |
| | When: |
| | Status: |
| | Completed Reality Date: |
| # 56 | What: |
| | How: |
| | Why: |
| | When: |
| | Status: |
| | Completed Reality Date: |

| # 57 | What: |
| | How: |
| | Why: |
| | When: |
| | Status: |
| | Completed Reality Date: |
| # 58 | What: |
| | How: |
| | Why: |
| | When: |
| | Status: |
| | Completed Reality Date: |
| # 59 | What: |
| | How: |
| | Why: |
| | When: |
| | Status: |
| | Completed Reality Date: |

## 20/20 Vision Dreams

| # 60 | What: |
| --- | --- |
| | How: |
| | Why: |
| | When: |
| | Status: |
| | Completed Reality Date: |
| # 61 | What: |
| | How: |
| | Why: |
| | When: |
| | Status: |
| | Completed Reality Date: |
| # 62 | What: |
| | How: |
| | Why: |
| | When: |
| | Status: |
| | Completed Reality Date: |

| # 63 | What: |
| | How: |
| | Why: |
| | When: |
| | Status: |
| | Completed Reality Date: |
| # 64 | What: |
| | How: |
| | Why: |
| | When: |
| | Status: |
| | Completed Reality Date: |
| # 65 | What: |
| | How: |
| | Why: |
| | When: |
| | Status: |
| | Completed Reality Date: |

## 20/20 Vision Dreams

| # 66 | What: |
| --- | --- |
| | How: |
| | Why: |
| | When: |
| | Status: |
| | Completed Reality Date: |
| # 67 | What: |
| | How: |
| | Why: |
| | When: |
| | Status: |
| | Completed Reality Date: |
| # 68 | What: |
| | How: |
| | Why: |
| | When: |
| | Status: |
| | Completed Reality Date: |

| # 69 | What: |
| | How: |
| | Why: |
| | When: |
| | Status: |
| | Completed Reality Date: |
| # 70 | What: |
| | How: |
| | Why: |
| | When: |
| | Status: |
| | Completed Reality Date: |
| # 71 | What: |
| | How: |
| | Why: |
| | When: |
| | Status: |
| | Completed Reality Date: |

| #72 | What: |
| | How: |
| | Why: |
| | When: |
| | Status: |
| | Completed Reality Date: |
| #73 | What: |
| | How: |
| | Why: |
| | When: |
| | Status: |
| | Completed Reality Date: |
| #74 | What: |
| | How: |
| | Why: |
| | When: |
| | Status: |
| | Completed Reality Date: |

| # 75 | What: |
|---|---|
| | How: |
| | Why: |
| | When: |
| | Status: |
| | Completed Reality Date: |
| # 76 | What: |
| | How: |
| | Why: |
| | When: |
| | Status: |
| | Completed Reality Date: |
| # 77 | What: |
| | How: |
| | Why: |
| | When: |
| | Status: |
| | Completed Reality Date: |

## 20/20 VISION DREAMS

| # 78 | What: |
| | How: |
| | Why: |
| | When: |
| | Status: |
| | Completed Reality Date: |
| # 79 | What: |
| | How: |
| | Why: |
| | When: |
| | Status: |
| | Completed Reality Date: |
| # 80 | What: |
| | How: |
| | Why: |
| | When: |
| | Status: |
| | Completed Reality Date: |

| # 81 | What: |
| | How: |
| | Why: |
| | When: |
| | Status: |
| | Completed Reality Date: |
| # 82 | What: |
| | How: |
| | Why: |
| | When: |
| | Status: |
| | Completed Reality Date: |
| # 83 | What: |
| | How: |
| | Why: |
| | When: |
| | Status: |
| | Completed Reality Date: |

| # 84 | What: |
| | How: |
| | Why: |
| | When: |
| | Status: |
| | Completed Reality Date: |
| # 85 | What: |
| | How: |
| | Why: |
| | When: |
| | Status: |
| | Completed Reality Date: |
| # 86 | What: |
| | How: |
| | Why: |
| | When: |
| | Status: |
| | Completed Reality Date: |

| # 87 | What: |
| | How: |
| | Why: |
| | When: |
| | Status: |
| | Completed Reality Date: |
| # 88 | What: |
| | How: |
| | Why: |
| | When: |
| | Status: |
| | Completed Reality Date: |
| # 89 | What: |
| | How: |
| | Why: |
| | When: |
| | Status: |
| | Completed Reality Date: |

| # 90 | What: |
|---|---|
| | How: |
| | Why: |
| | When: |
| | Status: |
| | Completed Reality Date: |
| # 91 | What: |
| | How: |
| | Why: |
| | When: |
| | Status: |
| | Completed Reality Date: |
| # 92 | What: |
| | How: |
| | Why: |
| | When: |
| | Status: |
| | Completed Reality Date: |

| # 93 | What: |
|---|---|
| | How: |
| | Why: |
| | When: |
| | Status: |
| | Completed Reality Date: |
| # 94 | What: |
| | How: |
| | Why: |
| | When: |
| | Status: |
| | Completed Reality Date: |
| # 95 | What: |
| | How: |
| | Why: |
| | When: |
| | Status: |
| | Completed Reality Date: |

## 20/20 VISION DREAMS

| # 96 | What: |
| --- | --- |
| | How: |
| | Why: |
| | When: |
| | Status: |
| | Completed Reality Date: |
| # 97 | What: |
| | How: |
| | Why: |
| | When: |
| | Status: |
| | Completed Reality Date: |
| # 98 | What: |
| | How: |
| | Why: |
| | When: |
| | Status: |
| | Completed Reality Date: |

| # 99 | What: |
| | How: |
| | Why: |
| | When: |
| | Status: |
| | Completed Reality Date: |
| # 100 | What: |
| | How: |
| | Why: |
| | When: |
| | Status: |
| | Completed Reality Date: |

# About the Author

Garnet Sheen Anthony Thompson was born in Jamaica and raised from birth by his maternal grandparents. Between the ages of 9 to 14 he lived with several different family units consisting of extended relatives and friends (including the Minister of a Church and his family); while his grandparents immigrated to Canada to establish new roots.

After finally meeting his biological father at the age of 27, he overcame tremendous self-doubt, social, and economic challenges through persistence,willpower, and with the support of compassionate relatives, mentors, and friends.

A trusted leader, husband, and father, Garnet is also a member of the executive team at a leading health and wellness company, which is rated amongst the top in the world. He possesses a deep desire and intention to be a legendary force for good, by bringing value to the marketplace and driving positive change in our world.

Garnet is the debut author of a new and powerful book, 20/20 Vision Dreams. This is an interactive book and journal focused on helping youthful individuals develop and sustain the attitude necessary to pursue, track, and live their dreams.

## Contact Information

**Twitter**

https://twitter.com/listof100dreams

**General Email**

listof100dreams@gmail.com

**Website**

garnetthompson.com

www.ingramcontent.com/pod-product-compliance
Lightning Source LLC
Chambersburg PA
CBHW060522100426
42743CB00009B/1406